WHY MEN CHEAT?

Hidden Voice

Copyright © 2025 by Hidden Voice.

All rights reserved. No part of this publication may be reproduced, distributed, or transmitted in any form or by any electronic or mechanical means, including information storage and retrieval systems, without a prior written permission from the publisher, except by reviewers, who may quote brief passages in a review, and certain other noncommercial uses permitted by the copyright law.

ISBN: 979-8-89228-420-2   (Paperback)
ISBN: 979-8-89228-421-9   (Hardcover)
ISBN: 979-8-89228-422-6   (eBook)

Book Ordering Information:
Atticus Publishing
548 Market St PMB 70756
San Francisco, CA 94104
(888) 208-9296
info@atticuspublishing.com
www.atticuspublishing.com

Printed in the United States of America

Contents

Introduction 1

Jane's Worldview 4
    The Spark of Love 4

Rumors and Heartbreak 6
The Weight of Betrayal 8
A Second Betrayal 10
Walking Away 13
Lessons in Love and Betrayal 14
Why Men Cheat? 15
    Faithful and Focused 15

The Cost of Emotional Isolation 16
A Nagging Wife and Its Impact 17
Two Roles, One Truth 18
Dissatisfaction and Desire 20
Boring sex life 21
A Taste of Something New 22
The Impact of an Unsupportive Partner 23
Boosting Pride Through Betrayal 24

Hurt People Hurt Others 27
Faithful or Simply Traditional? 29
What Sets Them Apart? 30

Conclusion: The Path to True Freedom 31

INTRODUCTION

Why do men cheat? It's a question that echoes through tearful nights, whispered in heartbreak, confusion, and anger. It's a question as old as love itself—one that carries the weight of pain, misunderstanding, and the stories we tell ourselves about what love should be. But behind the heartbreak lies a tangle of emotions, insecurities, social expectations, and choices that deserve a closer look.

This book doesn't claim to have all the answers, but it does aim to uncover the truth. Through raw, unfiltered stories and honest reflections, we'll explore the complex reasons behind infidelity. Not to justify it, but to understand it.

Cheating isn't just a moral failing—it's often a sign of something deeper. Loneliness, unmet needs, emotional disconnection, or even the pressure of societal norms can push someone to cross that line. By peeling back these layers, this book creates a space for open conversations, healing, and growth.

Together, we'll dig into the roots of betrayal, examine how relationships can rise or fall in its wake, and explore what it takes to build love on a foundation of trust, understanding, and honesty.

This isn't a story about pointing fingers. It's about discovery—about looking into the messy, imperfect corners of human relationships and finding a way forward.

So let's begin this journey. Together.

All good stories start with the phrase "Once upon a time." And so, allow me to begin the same way:

Once upon a time, there was a friend of mine named Jane (not her real name). Jane had an experience in her relationship so profoundly teachable that she begged me to share it.

This is her account, as told by Jane herself.

Jane's Worldview

The Spark of Love

Love is a beautiful thing—a warm fire crackling in the chilly winter gloom. When I started campus, I was eager to embrace everything life had to offer—young, strong, and full of zeal. The campus welcome party was nothing short of magical, and it was there that I met Mark.

It was love at first sight, clear as day. His gaze locked with mine, and something shifted. His glassy blue eyes held a depth that pulled me in, and his lips—ripe, pink, and moist—seemed to whisper promises even before he spoke. His mustache danced gently above his upper lip, teasing a smile that made my heart race.

I swear, I broke skin just from his glance. Any woman knows that electrifying moment when a man's look can set your entire body ablaze.

Our chats quickly turned into long, late-night phone calls. Brunches became breakfast and dinner dates. Sleepovers transitioned into mornings with breakfast in bed. Late-night walks evolved into shared candlelit baths in scented rooms.

It was a time to live, love, and be loved—or so I thought.

I saw no one else, touched no one else, and thought of no one else but Mark. He filled every corner of my mind, every empty space in my heart, and even in my blind spots, he was somehow always visible.

I was in love.

Damn it!

I was raised in a devout Christian home. My mother instilled Christian values and taught us the essence of being a lady, ensuring we always knew when we were wrong. My dad, our protector, kept us at a careful distance from the boys at church. An arm's length was as close as I ever got.

Mark found me whole. He swept me off my feet, leaving no stone unturned. I gave myself to him because, in my heart, I truly believed I had found the one.

Rumors and Heartbreak

Everything was merry and jolly until our third year. We were seniors now, with only one year left to graduate. I kept dreaming about how he might propose to me—how he would ask for my hand in marriage.

Then came the rumors.

Some of my friends began telling me that Mark was sleeping around.

They even warned me to be careful not to catch a disease. My Mark? You must be joking. My Mark loves me, and I love him too. Their words fell on deaf ears. I was love-struck. And love is blind—apparently deaf too.

And then, I walked in.

There he was—Mark—entangled in a moment I couldn't unsee. My best friend. My best friend. The air left my lungs as if I had been punched. I stood there, frozen, unable to reconcile what my eyes were screaming at me.

I saw him. I saw them. Their betrayal played out in stark clarity, no shadows to obscure the truth. My heart shattered into a thousand irretrievable pieces.

How do you unsee something so cruel? How do you turn a blind eye when the truth is staring back at you with such merciless clarity?

I confronted Mark, my heart shattered beyond repair. He said little, his silence cutting deeper than words, until he coldly remarked that I should "know my place." His words echoed in my mind, replaying endlessly as I struggled to make sense of the betrayal. In the end, I chose to forgive him—because, after all, even the Good Book teaches us to forgive and forget.

The Weight of Betrayal

By April, I noticed something troubling. I hadn't seen my monthlies for two full moons. Fear gripped me as I faced the possibility—I might be pregnant. In my confusion and panic, I sought advice from the man I believed would one day be my husband.

"I'm NOT ready to be a father. I ain't raising no kids. I'm only a student. You better handle that," he said.

His words cut deeper than a sacrificial knife. He didn't care.

I drove myself to the hospital, tears flooding my eyes. This was our first major fight. At the hospital, the news hit me—I was five weeks pregnant.

Shame consumed me. I felt as though I'd disappointed the man I thought was my future husband, ashamed for allowing myself to get pregnant. Without thinking much, and overwhelmed by despair, I did what I thought any girl in my position would do.

I terminated the pregnancy.

I felt regret. I felt shame. I felt fear. I felt lost. And I grieved. I had lost. I was sick to my stomach. I hated myself.

After a week of crying alone, drowning in regret, I went back to Mark to apologize—for the "mistake" of getting pregnant. He forgave me. He even said he was glad I had made the "wise decision," or so he believed.

A Second Betrayal

A week later, I decided to surprise him at his house. But instead of joy, I found him in bed with another woman. I froze, trembling as confusion clouded my mind. Tears blurred my vision, and I bolted out the door, crying. He followed—half-naked—and pulled me into his chest.

"I'm sorry," he whispered.

I kept crying in his arms.

I had endured too much to let a "two-time mistake" break us apart.

For the next month, Mark seemed different. He wasn't glued to his phone. He gave me the attention I craved, taking me on dates every chance he got. He seemed reformed—or so I thought.

Then August came—my birthday month. Mark threw me the biggest birthday party I'd ever had. I felt happy. I felt special. Everything seemed perfect.

Until it wasn't.

I found him in the bathroom, once again degrading our relationship. He didn't even notice I was standing there, watching. I let him be.

In that moment, all the pain I had buried—the loss of my firstborn child, the memories, the agony, the fear, the shame—came rushing back. I stumbled to the nearest sink and threw up.

Later that night, as I lay next to Mark in bed, all I could feel was disgust. He reeked of infidelity, a sexual rot that seemed to cling to him. Or was it just in my head?

Was I not good enough? What did he see in these other women that I lacked? Didn't he find me pure and whole? Had I done something wrong, or was I simply not good enough?

For the first time, I contemplated murder—or death. It was either of the two. I had never been suicidal, but that night, I almost felt what death tasted like.

I had never been aggressive; I could barely swat a fly. But I wanted him gone. I wished him dead. And yet, I also felt dead inside. The only thing I lacked was the courage to take my own life.

Night turned into morning, and I didn't say a word about it.

I had been a good girlfriend. I hoped to be an even better wife.

But why would anyone cheat on the birthday girl?

Walking Away

I endured eight similar instances of being cheated on before I finally found the strength to walk away.

There's a saying that all men cheat, but if he loves you enough, you'll never find out. I'm not sure how true that is, but I do know that every man is different, and everyone should be held accountable for their actions.

Lessons in Love and Betrayal

It's this experience—along with the stories shared by other women brave enough to open up—that inspired the writing of this book.

This book is a journey into the social concepts behind why men become unfaithful. It is an open discussion meant to help women better understand men. It combines the perspectives of women on why they believe men cheat with the raw, honest realities shared by men about why they actually did cheat.

WHY MEN CHEAT?

Faithful and Focused

Are there good men in the world? Yes!

There are good men all over the world—faithful to one woman, focused, disciplined, and dedicated. However, it's important to remember this: within every good, there is always the potential for bad.

The Cost of Emotional Isolation

Among the loneliest people in the world are men. Bound by the weight of their many duties, they rarely experience heartfelt intimacy. Yet, we are all social beings. A man walking through life without a companion often loses hope or focus, which can sometimes lead him to seek fulfillment elsewhere.

It is a deeply ingrained and misguided belief that men are not meant to be emotional. The truth is, men are often more sentimental than women. But the societal expectation that a man must always appear strong teaches them to bury their feelings. Emotions, too often, are seen as a sign of weakness.

What the world truly needs are men who embrace their capacity to feel and express emotion. The real mark of strength lies in a man who has found resilience and authenticity within himself. Men who are in touch with their emotions not only make better partners but also become exceptional fathers.

A Nagging Wife and Its Impact

Men are creatures of comfort. They thrive in the ease of life and are often considered big children. Every man loves a quiet, peaceful home and a woman who is in touch with her feminine side.

Men are natural problem-solvers. Progress, for them, means solving one issue and moving to the next. A nagging woman is often the easiest victim of infidelity, as her husband may look for "side show" women to meet his needs—better known as side chicks.

There is nothing more unsettling for a man than being unable to find peace of mind in his own household. Nothing is as disappointing as being unable to find peace through his partner. A woman who brings peace, joy, comfort, and satisfaction will effortlessly occupy a man's heart.

Two Roles, One Truth

In the world of infidelity, side chicks often play distinct roles:

- The Future Wife: A side chick with the potential to replace the current wife.
- The Marriage Enforcer: A side chick who temporarily sustains the man during a time of need but has no future prospects with him. She unintentionally helps the man appreciate and love his wife even more.

No one loves harder than a man who has just cheated, which is why some people say, "Side chicks sustain marriages."

Everyone has a role to play in life. So, please, let's respect them all.

Only a man knows which woman plays which role in his life. Most married men with a "marriage enforcer" side chick will deny her existence and fight to protect their marriage or wife if caught.

However, if the man has a "future wife" type of side chick, the situation becomes more complicated. He is faced with a difficult choice, and more often than not, the wife ends up being divorced.

Once again, don't shoot the messenger—aim for the sender. I'm only the messenger.

Dissatisfaction and Desire

Human beings have five basic needs. Men, however, have a sixth: sex. This is one of the most controversial topics and a leading reason why men step out of their relationships.

The quality and frequency of sex in any relationship significantly influence how couples interact with one another. Many married men—or men in relationships—are dissatisfied with the frequency of their sexual interactions with their partners.

Who is to blame? Well, that's a personal question. But if the shoe fits...

As always, I am just here to verbalize the recurring question: Is a man who is sexually dissatisfied justified in cheating?

It is also worth remembering that men often equate sexual interactions with intimacy.

Boring sex life

Does the quality of sex matter? This topic may have been partially addressed earlier, but it's worth delving deeper.

What constitutes a boring sex life, and what does an engaging, captivating one look like? These are essential questions to consider, especially when monotony begins to creep into the bedroom.

Interestingly, most women who are dissatisfied in bed tend to keep it a secret, while most men often feel satisfied—though their primary concern seems to be frequency.

This raises further questions: Would we say that women are justified in stepping out if they are dissatisfied in bed? And is every man who feels dissatisfied in bed justified in cheating?

A Taste of Something New

Are all women the same? This is a common phrase, and even I don't know how to answer it. People differ in their character, personality, beliefs, opinions, and even physical appearance. No two individuals are identical. Even identical twins have their differences.

When men cheat and claim they are looking for "something different," what exactly is the "difference" they are referring to? And does this justify their actions?

There's also a concept often referred to as "falling out of love." This is when someone believes they are no longer in love or attracted to their spouse and ends up cheating under the guise of "falling out of love."

This kind of thinking largely depends on how a couple defines love and how well they understand it.

The Impact of an Unsupportive Partner

Some women can be selfish. An unsupportive wife is one who prioritizes her own needs or feelings above those of her man—especially when he needs her most. This lack of support can vary depending on the situation, the issue, or the specific needs of the man.

This behavior often mirrors that of a nagging wife. In the end, both types of women frequently find themselves being cheated on.

The reality is, there is always someone willing to treat your man better than you do. And the reverse is just as true.

Boosting Pride Through Betrayal

This perspective offers a fresh philosophy on why men cheat. Men are inherently egocentric beings, and their pride serves as their lifeline.

A happy husband takes pride in his wife—particularly in how she handles herself in challenging situations, such as when another man is being overly familiar or flirtatious. A good wife establishes clear boundaries, making it known—both privately and publicly—that such behavior is unacceptable. Loyalty demonstrated in the shadows is loyalty nonetheless.

Men are naturally possessive. They take pride in what they have, and if they don't possess it yet, they often strive relentlessly to achieve it. A man frequently mentors or guides his partner to align with the shared standards and goals he envisions for their future. Men are hard workers by nature. When pursuing a woman, they invest considerable effort into the relationship, finding immense pride in their accomplishment. For men, effort is identity; their sweat defines them.

Even in the bedroom, where men often take on the active role, they derive fulfillment from their sense of achievement—how deeply they've connected with and satisfied their partner. For many men, the bedroom becomes the ultimate ego boost, tying their sexual vitality to their overall sense of self.

When a man's ego is nurtured within his household, he feels empowered to take on the world, regardless of his occupation or status. However, a man's ego is not static—it fluctuates based on circumstances and the seasons of life.

Men with a shaky ego at home often seek external validation. This is where cheating—or "stepping out"—can come into play. It serves as a misguided attempt to remind themselves that they are still hunters, still the roaring lions of the jungle. This behavior temporarily reaffirms their sense of pride and shifts their outlook on life. Some men return to their responsibilities with renewed vigor, loving their partners more passionately or avoiding conflict entirely—sometimes as a reaction to a nagging partner.

However, a wife or girlfriend who fails to positively influence her man's mental and emotional space may inadvertently create room for infidelity in the relationship. This dynamic can lead to glorified side relationships, fractured homes, and broken families.

Hurt People Hurt Others

Insecurity is an undercurrent in many relationships, often subtle but deeply impactful. For men grappling with profound self-doubt, insecurity can sometimes pave the way to infidelity. When a partner harbors these hidden wounds, the relationship may falter, and cheating becomes a misguided attempt to fill an emotional void.

These insecurities often stem from scars—doubt seeded by past hurts, unresolved pain from previous relationships, or the absence of a nurturing upbringing. Growing up without a steady figure—a father, a guardian, or a mentor—can leave a young man unsure of himself, his worth, and his place in the world. Broken people, as the saying goes, often hurt others.

The depth of insecurity varies, but its effects can be profound—unsettled thoughts, nagging fears, and unanswered questions that create restlessness. A restless mind, searching for peace or validation, may wander, seeking solace in the wrong places.

Yet, a partner has the power to counter these doubts. Being present—not just physically, but emotionally—and living fully in the moment can create a sense of safety and security. This reassurance is a foundation on which a relationship can thrive, even in the face of life's uncertainties.

Understanding and addressing insecurity isn't just about healing one person—it's about nurturing the connection that binds two people together.

Faithful or Simply Traditional?

Different men have different reasons for being polygamous. Historically, polygamy has even been used as a way to prevent cheating. In polygamous communities, each member contributes to the greater good of the larger family unit.

But this raises an important question: Can a polygamous man be considered a cheater?

What Sets Them Apart?

In our analysis, faithful men tend to share some common features:

- They are purpose-driven.
- They exhibit discipline and self-control.
- They have a strong belief system.
- They are family-oriented.

These are just a few traits to consider. We'll explore this and much more on our next journey together.

Conclusion: The Path to True Freedom

The upbringing of a stable family is the primary objective of every man.

A man without purpose is like a stray bullet—eventually, even a tree becomes a target. Contentment in a man reflects true maturity. Everyone has a choice: to be content with what they have or where they are. And if not, then brighten the corner where you are.

The grass isn't greener on the other side; it's greener where you water it. Bettering what you already have is the essence of growth in human life. Otherwise, it's all an endless pit of dissatisfaction.

Discipline shapes character, and character defines the man. Every man has an appetite. Some give in to every tempting bite they see, becoming slaves to their own desires. A man who cannot control his appetite is a slave to his emotions.

True freedom lies in discipline.

www.ingramcontent.com/pod-product-compliance
Ingram Content Group UK Ltd.
Pitfield, Milton Keynes, MK11 3LW, UK
UKHW040608060225
454636UK00030B/16